Let's get moving in the jungle

Emma Lynch

Heinemann
LIBRARY

Little Nippers

www.heinemann.co.uk/library
Visit our website to find out more information about **Heinemann Library** books.

To order:
☎ Phone 44 (0) 1865 888066
▤ Send a fax to 44 (0) 1865 314091
▢ Visit the Heinemann Bookshop at www.heinemann.co.uk/library to browse our catalogue and order online.

First published in Great Britain by Heinemann Library, Halley Court, Jordan Hill, Oxford OX2 8EJ, part of Harcourt Education.
Heinemann is a registered trademark of Harcourt Education Ltd.

© Harcourt Education Ltd 2004
The moral right of the proprietor has been asserted.

Editorial: Jilly Attwood and Kate Bellamy
Design: Jo Hinton-Malivoire
Models made by: Jo Brooker
Picture Research: Rosie Garai and Emma Lynch
Production: Séverine Ribierre

Originated by Dot Gradations
Printed and bound in China by South China Printing Company

ISBN 0 431 16477 0 (hardback)
08 07 06 05 04
10 9 8 7 6 5 4 3 2 1

ISBN 0 431 16482 7 (paperback)
08 07 06 05 04
10 9 8 7 6 5 4 3 2 1

British Library Cataloguing in Publication Data
Lynch, Emma
Let's get moving... in the jungle
591.5'09152
A full catalogue record for this book is available from the British Library.

Acknowledgements
The publishers would like to thank the following for permission to reproduce photographs: Bruce Coleman p. 6; Corbis pp. 13 (Michael & Patricia Fogden), 21 (Kevin Schafer), 12a (Paul A. Souders); Corbis/Royalty Free pp. 4a, 7a, 11, 19; Getty Images pp. 5, 8, 14, 18, 22 (Digital Vision), 9, 10, 15 (photodisc); Harcourt Education Ltd pp. 4b, 5b, 6b, 7b, 8b, 9b, 10b, 11b, 12b, 13b, 14b, 15b, 16b, 17b, 18b, 19b, 20, 21b, 23 (Tudor Photography); NHPA p. 16 (Stephen Dalton); Oxford Scientific Films p. 20.

Cover photograph reproduced with permission of NHPA/Martin Wendler.

Our thanks to Annie Davy for her assistance in the preparation of this book.

Every effort has been made to contact copyright holders of any material reproduced in this book. Any omissions will be rectified in subsequent printings if notice is given to the publishers.

This paper used to print this book comes from sustainable resources.

Contents

Enter the jungle

Creep into the jungle like a **prowling** tiger.

Reach up high
to touch the
sky like the
tallest
jungle tree.

5

On the jungle floor

March like the army ants along the floor.

Left, right, left, right, keep in line!

Scuttle like a spider through the jungle plants.

Up a tree

Slope along **slowly**
like a sloth.

Slither and slide like a **slippery**, scaly snake.

Along a branch

Can you hang upside-down like a bat from a branch?

In among the leaves

Trail slowly like a vine from tree to tree.

vine

Flutter gently
through the leaves
like a butterfly.

At the treetops

Who can? You can.
Fly like a toucan.

beak

Clamber through the branches
like a multi-coloured macaw.

Over the jungle

Now rise into the skies
and soar like a bird.

Climbing down

Swing like an ape down through the trees.

Wheeee! Look at me!

Or **leap** like a tree frog from branch to branch.

Back on the ground

Crawl like a coati, sniffing for grubs.

Hop on a log like the cock of the rock.

Rest

Even crocodiles get tired, so find a warm spot to have a rest.

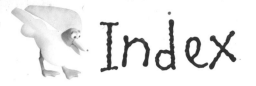

Index

The end

Notes for adults

Let's get moving! explores the many different ways humans can move and encourages children to take part in physical activity. *Let's get moving!* also supports children's growing knowledge and understanding of the wider world, introducing them to different plants and animals and the way they move and grow. Used together, the books will enable comparison of different movements and of a variety of habitats and the animals that live in them.

The key curriculum Early Learning Goals relevant to this series are:

Early Learning Goals for movement
• Move with confidence, imagination and in safety
• Move with control and coordination
Early Learning Goals for sense of space
• Show awareness of space, self and of others
Early Learning Goals for exploration and investigation
• Find out about and identify some features of living things

This book introduces the reader to a range of movements used by animals in the jungle. It will also help children extend their vocabulary as they hear new words like *prowl, scales, hover* and *soar*. You may like to introduce and explain other new words yourself, like *rainforest, habitat* and *endangered*.

Additional information

Most living things can move. Humans and many other animals have skeletons and muscles to support and protect their bodies and to help them move. Jungles usually refer to tropical rainforests, which are found near the equator. They are home to millions of plants and animals. Rainforests have a typical weather pattern of hot, sunny mornings with rain in the afternoons, making them an ideal place for plant growth.

Follow-up activities

• Can the children think of some other jungle animals? Try to copy their movements.
• Learn and sing songs about the jungle, such as 'Down in the jungle'.
• Talk about what it would be like to live in the jungle. What would they need and want to take with them?